Ballet:
A Pictorial History

Walter Terry

VNR VAN NOSTRAND REINHOLD COMPANY
New York Cincinnati Toronto London Melbourne

Van Nostrand Reinhold Company Regional Offices: New York Cincinnati
Chicago Millbrae Dallas
Van Nostrand Reinhold Company International Offices: London Toronto Melbourne

Designed by Jean Callan King
Printed by Mahony & Roese Inc.
Bound by Publishers Book Bindery, Inc.
Published by Van Nostrand Reinhold Company, 450 West 33rd Street, N. Y., N.Y. 10001
Published simultaneously in Canada by Van Nostrand Reinhold Company Ltd.

1 3 5 7 9 11 13 15 16 14 12 10 8 6 4 2

Contents

2. A Gallery of Modern Stars 33

Seconde Journée

Theatre fait dans la mesme allée, sur lequel la Comédie, et le Ballet
de la Princesse d'Elide furent representéz.

The Royal Beginning
(1581-1681)

The dance is one of the oldest of artistic expressions. Since the earliest of times people have shown their feelings and acted out stories through rhythmic and patterned movements of the body.

This book is about the ballet, which is like no other form of dance. Many people from all over the world have helped to make it what it is, but its name is traced to an Italian word, *ballare*, which means "to dance," and its roots are in the *banquet-fêtes* held by the Italian royalty to celebrate special occasions.

These fêtes—"feasts"—were large parties in which dancing was combined with the serving of food. Neptune, the ancient god of the sea, and his attendants would bring in the fish course. Diana, goddess of hunting, and her maidens would dance in with a huge platter laden with venison and wild boar to serve the guests. And so the celebration went, on through dessert. Everyone could look and eat at the same time.

Queen Catherine of France

Catherine de Médici, born in Italy in 1519, was a member of the Italian nobility but became Queen of France when she married Henry II. Catherine is known to have been an excellent dancer and is said to have commanded the first ballet—the *Ballet Comique de la Reine*. For it she ordered special painted sets and music to go with the dances arranged by her choreographer. (A choreographer is like the director of a play or motion picture—he decides how the dancers are to be arranged on stage and what steps they will perform.) This first ballet, performed in 1581 for ten thousand guests, was not what we now think of as ballet, but it was the beginning. Queen Catherine separated the eating from the watching, and her dance told a continuous story—that of Circe, the pretty witch. It took five hours to play this tale in dancing, music, and poetry.

The *Ballet Comique de la Reine* was important not just to France. In the audience were important visitors from kingdoms all over Europe, and many of them wrote home to their own queens and kings. Eventually other big capitals had their own court ballets, which in time would change into professional ballet companies. For almost three hundred years, however, Paris remained the capital of ballet.

Kings and queens and princes were the first to support ballet. Sometimes they sat on their thrones and watched dances performed not in a theater but in a palace, as shown in the facing page. And sometimes they even danced themselves, like Queen Catherine, below, wearing a long necklace and with big polka dots on her sleeves. She liked to dance with other courtly performers.

Right, King Louis XIV of France, who was an accomplished dancer. *Below,* bronze statuettes of Lafontaine, the world's first ballerina (left), and one of her partners. The time? Almost 300 years ago!

PHOTOGRAPH BY LOUIS PERES

King Louis XIV

About sixty years after Queen Catherine's historic ballet, Louis XIV ascended the throne of France. He too liked to dance. In the big ballets presented in his palaces and castles he often took various parts. His favorite role was that of the Greek god Apollo. In ancient days, the Greeks believed that Apollo carried the sun in his chariot as he rode across the sky. Perhaps that is why King Louis also liked to be called the "Sun King."

Louis XIV did more for ballet than just dance himself whenever he wanted to: he started the first ballet school in the world where any young person, not just princes and princesses, could learn to be dancers. He called it the *Académie Royale de Danse* ("Royal Academy of Dancing"). It began in Paris in 1661.

The dancing teachers engaged by King Louis held their classes in palace rooms, where the first non-royal students began to prepare for the professional stage at the Paris Opéra. In 1669, the king set up a royal academy of music, and two years later he combined the two into one big school where dancers and musicians could get the best training to be found anywhere in the world.

In the performances at the royal court, ladies as well as gentlemen took part, but in the public theaters the roles of girls and women were played by young boys—perhaps because parents were not sure that it was proper for their daughters to dance on the stage. (This was also true in England, where all the heroines of Shakespeare's plays were played by boys.) But the custom changed when King Louis began his school. Girls as well as boys studied ballet to prepare themselves for the public theater. Before many years had passed both girls and boys from the Royal Academy were ready to dance in operas, which began to have many ballets in them. Some of the young dancers were probably very good, but it was twenty years after the founding of the Academy that France presented to the world the first great ballerina.

Lafontaine

The Royal Academy's first ballerina to become known throughout the world was a beautiful girl with just one name, Lafontaine. Her appearance was quite different from today's dancers. She wore high heels because toe shoes had not been invented. Her skirts were floor-length, and on her head she wore a wig covered with many kinds of jewels and toys, sometimes even little ships. In such heavy dress, it was just about all anyone could do to stand up, but Lafontaine danced. Her début was in Paris in 1681. The steps she did were simple, but everyone in Paris loved her. Her audiences thought she was so wonderful that they called her "Queen of the Dance."

Ballet Becomes Professional

(1681-1730)

With Lafontaine's great success in a ballet called *Le Triomphe de L'Amour* ("The Triumph of Love"), public interest in ballet grew. The form of the spectacle, however, remained much the same as in Queen Catherine's day: a story was told in scenes that were acted out with words and pantomime and songs. Between these scenes were what the French called *entrées;* they were little dances. In *Triomphe* there were twenty such *entrées*.

Dancing with Lafontaine were three other girls trained to be professional dancers at the royal academy, but none of them became as well known as she.

Marie Subligny

The next *première danseuse* ("first dancer," female) at the Paris Opéra was Mademoiselle Marie Subligny. She was elevated to that position when Mademoiselle Lafontaine retired from the stage to spend the rest of her life in a convent. We know very little about Mademoiselle Subligny, but we do know that she went to London to dance for the English—and that they liked her very much. It would then seem that she was the first to go "on tour." Since that time it has become customary for accomplished dancers to be invited to perform away from home. At first only stars traveled, and then only to nearby countries. Eventually, however, there were tours to Russia and to America. And still later entire companies took their ballets around the world. Even though we are not sure how Mademoiselle Subligny danced, we can thank her for the precedent of taking ballet "on tour."

Françoise Prévost

In ballet, as in history, not everything happens at once. There are big occasions, famous kings, important presidents, and world-famous ballerinas—but there are also the "in-betweens." You might call Françoise Prévost something of an in-between. She was a very good dancer—so good that she was the *première danseuse* at the Paris Opéra for almost thirty years.

Two "Maries"—friendly rivals: Marie Camargo (facing page) and Marie Sallé (below).

Prévost was both a dancer and an actress. She is said to have known more about ballet and to have been able to do more dance steps than Lafontaine or Subligny, who both came before her. The *entrées* in the opera spectacles were still the court dances of the day (pavanes, gigues, passepieds, chaconnes); but she danced them so beautifully—"with fluent elegance," it was said—that composers of music wrote especially for her. As an actress-dancer she once performed the last act of a tragedy without speaking a word. She and another dancer did the entire scene in pantomime, and so effectively that some persons in the audience cried.

Prévost was also a good ballet teacher. When she grew old and retired, two of her pupils took her place at the Paris Opéra. They were Marie Camargo and Marie Sallé.

Marie Camargo

Many young girls who study ballet hope one day to become ballerinas. Only a very few of them do. One was Marie Camargo. After the Royal Academy in Paris with Prévost she became a member of the *corps de ballet*—the ballet troupe—at the Paris Opéra. This meant that she was only one of many dancers performing on stage at the same time. Her opportunity to become a star came one day when the *premier danseur* (or first male dancer) was nowhere to be found when the time came for his solo. Marie ran on stage and made up a dance as she went along to the music meant for the male dancer. She was a great success, and she became an outstanding ballerina.

Camargo did not like the long dresses and the high heels that Lafontaine and earlier ballerinas had worn. Therefore she cut her skirts shorter, so that she could do more steps and the audience could see them. She also took off her heels so that she could spring into the air in the manner of the *premier danseur*. She became noted for her daring—so much so that shoes, dresses, hats, and even omelets were named after her, *à la Camargo*. In our picture of Camargo, you will still see high heels, but you will notice that her skirts are shorter than those worn before her time.

Marie Sallé

Another pupil of Françoise Prévost whose inventions in ballet helped to shape its direction was also named Marie—Marie Sallé. One great difference between the two Maries was that Camargo invented ballet steps, while Sallé invented new ballets. Marie Sallé was the first woman to become a choreographer. The directors of the Paris Opéra where she danced did not want a woman choreographer, so she went to London. There she presented her new ballet in 1734. It was called *Pygmalion* and was based on an old, old fairy tale. Sallé became as famous in England as Marie Camargo had in Paris—though no one named an omelet after her!

A Century of Development (1730-1830)

Marie Allard, successor at the Paris Opéra to Camargo and Sallé, was a fine dancer, but the two that preceded her outshone her in fame, and the dancer who followed her earned greater acclaim. That dancer was Guimard, Allard's understudy, who, when the star injured her foot, replaced her in the role of Terpsichore (the Muse of Dancing) in an old and popular opera-ballet called *Les Fêtes Grecques et Romaines*. The choreographer Noverre has said that this was one of only four old-time ballets that met his own requirements for making dramatic sense. Guimard, Noverre's pupil, was an instant success in this, and later her teacher said, "She put expression and feeling into all her movements."

This was a time—1730 through 1830—when ballet developed slowly. The number of steps increased, but it was a matter of growing rather than changing. There were some new ideas, however: unmasking and exotic storytelling.

Previously dancers had always worn masks on stage, but as ballet tended to become more dramatic, or closer to acting, the masks were removed to allow the dancer to express emotions with his own face as well as through gesture. Gaetan Vestris, the greatest male dancer of this period, was the first to take off the mask. As a very young man, Gaetan danced a few times at the royal court with Sallé. His son, Auguste Vestris (Auguste's mother was Marie Allard), was the teacher of some of the most famous dancers and choreographers of the next great, and very different, age of ballet. So it is that the stories and steps and styles of ballet are passed along from one generation to another.

Ballet takes place not only on the stage with dancers but also behind the scenes with teachers and choreographers. The ballet in which Gaetan Vestris unmasked was made by the most important choreographer in France, Jean Georges Noverre.

Jean Georges Noverre started out as a dancer but became more interested in creating dances. Since he was just making a name for himself when Camargo and Sallé were about to retire, he worked mostly with dancers younger than they. Noverre allowed Vestris to unmask because he wished ballet to be more than just steps, and gesture to be something more realistic than the stylized motions for anger or love and laughter that had characterized pantomime.

Facing page, a dramatic scene from ballet of the 1700s, with Marie Allard, star of the Paris Opéra, who became the mother of the great male dancer Auguste Vestris; and Jean Dauberval, whom we know today as the choreographer of a great comedy-ballet, *La Fille Mal Gardée*.

Madeleine Guimard

Jean Georges Noverre

Gaetan Vestris, the greatest male dancer of his time, in a dramatic scene (with Mlles. Bacelli and Simonetti) from Noverre's ballet *Jason and Medea*. This was a very important ballet because it was the first one in which dancers did not wear masks on stage.

All that Noverre learned about dancing, acting, and music he put into what he called "action ballets." He had studied acting with the English actor David Garrick and had learned much about music from the German composer Christoph Gluck. David Garrick had such respect for Noverre's efforts that he called him the "Shakespeare of the dance." Noverre's book *Letters on Dancing and Ballets* (1760) was as important a contribution to the development of ballet as a new ballerina would have been. He did not live to see the Romantic magic ballets, but his action ballets pointed the way to the new era.

Noverre was not interested in just making up steps or having his dancers do difficult tricks. He wanted to tell a story in dance movements combined with true-to-life gestures. So successful was he with his ballet-dramas that he was praised by dramatists and composers as well as by dancers.

The Romantic Age of Ballet (1830-1870)

Marie Taglioni, the greatest ballerina of the Romantic age of Ballet, in *L'Ombre* ("The Shadow"), with Antonio Guerra. This is a lovely, idealized lithograph by Bouvier, but actually the rose was made of metal and Taglioni's toe was firmly fixed in it.

Until the nineteenth century, Greek myths and classical opera provided the main source of stories for ballet. Thus this early era is sometimes called the Classical age of ballet. The Romantic age marks a turning-away from these overworked and overly familiar stories to books and tales which were called "romances." In these, the world of the imagination was glorified. Magic was almost always mixed up with love, and ordinary people were involved with witches, elves, and sprites. In one ballet, you might find a Scottish boy and girl participating in an adventure with fairy-tale sylphides who have wings and fly about in the woods. In another, a girl will turn into a wili, a sprite that has wings and dances only in the moonlight, or into Ondine, who came out of the sea. The introduction of *pointe*, or standing on the very tips of the toes, enhanced the Romantic age in ballet: When on *pointe* the ballerina seemed to belong to a world somehow beyond the reach of ordinary people who kept their feet flat on the ground.

During this period dancers began to travel more and more. Paris was still the ballet center of the world, but other countries, including America, had well-established ballet troupes of their own. The star female dancer began to be known by the Italian title, "ballerina." A *ballerina* is a star dancer in a company. A *prima ballerina* is the "first," the leading woman in a ballet company. A *prima ballerina assoluta* is "absolutely the first"—not only in a company, but also in the entire country.

Marie Taglioni

When Marie Taglioni began her career, ballet already had a long history. Camargo and Sallé had retired from the stage seventy years earlier, and ballerinas had been dancing on *pointe* for about thirty years. But they had not been able to accomplish a variety of steps on their toes because in those days the shoes were too soft. And so Marie Taglioni made an important innovation. She darned her shoes with extra thread on the sides and tip to give her toes extra support. This enabled her to make dancing on *pointe* as beautiful to see as poetry is to hear. Her father, Philippe, choreographed many of her ballets, and the one that made her the greatest ballerina of her day was *La Sylphide*. It was first performed in Paris at the Opéra in 1832.

15

Fanny Elssler

Marie Taglioni's performances were delicate and dainty, and people liked to see her in the role of a fairy being, such as a sylphide. Fanny Elssler was also a great favorite at the Paris Opera during this time, but her dancing was very different. Fanny was fiery. Audiences liked to see her dance lively ballets based on Italian and Spanish stories. In 1840 Fanny came to America, the first great European ballerina to do so. On one occasion when she was in Washington, D.C., Congress closed its doors during the afternoon because so many senators and congressmen wanted to attend her matinee. An American dancer, George Washington Smith, was frequently her partner during her American tour.

Grisi, Cerrito, and Grahn

Carlotta Grisi was born in Italy and became a famous ballerina at the Paris Opéra. She combined the fairylike lightness of Taglioni with the liveliness of Elssler. In 1841 she performed a ballet created especially for her by the choreographer Jean Coralli and her husband, the dancer Jules Perrot. It was called *Giselle*. In the first act Giselle is seen as a happy, healthy, laughing girl. In the second act, she is a ghost flitting and flying in the forest at night. Carlotta danced both Giselles with equal magnificence, proving her versatility.

Fanny Cerrito was another popular ballerina at this time who was born in Italy. One of her most famous ballets was *Ondine*, in which she was the daughter of the Queen of the Waters—a nymph of the sea who fell in love with a fisherman and tried to live on dry land. She could not, and died. Fanny's favorite partner was her husband, Arthur Saint-Leon, who was also a choreographer.

Facing page, Fanny Elssler (left) and Carlotta Grisi; *right*, Fanny Cerrito. Fanny Elssler, from Austria, was Marie Taglioni's greatest rival. Fans used to think of Marie as a "creature of the air," Fanny as a "creature of the earth." Fanny is shown in an earthy Cracovienne from *La Gypsy*. Ballet followers in the early 1800s often thought that Carlotta Grisi, the very first ballerina to dance *Giselle*, combined the airiness of Taglioni with the earthiness of Elssler. Another famous ballerina of the Romantic Age was Fanny Cerrito; she was also a choreographer. She is shown in the popular Shadow Dance from *Ondine*.

The fifth *prima ballerina* of the Romantic age
was Denmark's Lucile Grahn. She was the first
to dance *La Sylphide* in Denmark, and the version she performed in 1836 is still danced today
all over the world. These were the days when
most ballets were about sylphides, elves, pixies,
and other fanciful creatures. Here is Grahn as a
special kind of fairy, a dryad, in *Eoline.*

Perhaps the most beautiful ballet picture in the
world is this lithograph by Chalon of the *Pas de
Quatre* with Gris, Taglioni, Grahn, and Cerrito.
They danced together in London by command of
Queen Victoria, and although they didn't like
each other very much, they had to do what the
queen had requested—and they managed to
smile.

18

During the Romantic age of ballet, the ballerina was the "queen of the dance," but men were important too. One of the most important was Jules Perrot, a wonderful dancer and also a choreographer. He was Carlotta Grisi's husband and designed all his wife's solos in *Giselle*, and it was he who persuaded four very temperamental stars to dance together in the *Pas de Quatre* for Queen Victoria.

Lucile Grahn, a native of Copenhagen, was the first great Danish ballerina in the long history of the Royal Danish Ballet. She danced in the light and airy tradition of Taglioni. She is important to the story of ballet because she danced *La Sylphide* as choreographed by August Bournonville. He had seen it performed in Paris, and when he went home to Copenhagen, he put it on the stage there with new music by a Danish composer. Although Taglioni's *La Sylphide* has long been forgotten, Bournonville's version is still being danced today.

One of the most famous performances of all time included all three of these ballerinas—Grisi, Cerrito, and Grahn—and also the great Taglioni. It was a *pas de quatre*—that is, "dance for four" —given in 1845 in London. This unprecedented performance was made at the command of Queen Victoria. Since the four ballerinas were rivals, each wanted the best dance, the most exciting steps, and the most important position. Grisi's husband, Perrot, was the choreographer, and he managed the very difficult job of planning the dance so that each ballerina danced the steps she did best. The dancers were pleased. The Queen was pleased. The audience was pleased. The artist Chalon was so pleased that he painted one of the most beautiful pictures in the history of ballet.

Augusta Maywood (near left) when she was known as "The Little Augusta," a child dancer; and her only rival, Mary Ann Lee (far left), the first American "Giselle." Both girls were from Philadelphia.

The First American Ballerinas

Europe, and especially Paris, was the center of the ballet, but young America also made its impact on ballet. In colonial times, teachers had come from Europe to instruct Americans in social dances and also in ballet. Way back in the 1790s, there was a very good American dancer named John Durang who danced for George Washington! Other dancers, trained in Philadelphia, New York, and other cities by French and English teachers, became expert; and America formed its first ballet companies. In the 1830s, when Taglioni and Elssler were the favorites of Paris, there were two little girls, Maywood and Lee, who were the toast of their hometown.

Augusta Maywood and Mary Ann Lee were rival child dancers from Philadelphia who became the first American ballerinas. The Little Augusta, as she was called, eventually journeyed to Paris, where she became the first American to study at the Royal Academy of Dancing and the first American to dance at the Paris Opéra. For the rest of her dancing life, she stayed in Europe.

Mary Ann Lee studied in Paris, although she did not dance at the Opéra. She learned the choreography for some of the great ballets, among them *Giselle*. She went back home and put on the stage in Boston the first *Giselle* ever seen in America. Her partner was George Washington Smith, also a Philadelphian, who had danced with Fanny Elssler herself when "the divine Fanny" toured America in the 1840s.

Ballet in Russia

Russia was active in ballet, and had ballet masters teaching it, as far back as 1735. Taglioni and Elssler, the great ballerinas of the Romantic age, visited there in the 1830s. Carlotta Grisi's husband, Jules Joseph Perrot, was for several years ballet master for the Russian Imperial Ballet, and there were many good Russian ballerinas during the early years. However, Russian ballet did not reach its peak until after the French choreographer Marius Petipa went there in 1847.

Marius Petipa

Before going to Russia, Petipa had danced in Paris with Fanny Elssler. Fanny had studied with Auguste Vestris, whose father, Gaetan, had danced with Sallé. Sallé had been a pupil of Prévost, and Prévost had been a student of Lafontaine. Again it is clear how ballet grew and developed in many lands, but had its roots in the same source.

Petipa had intended to stay in Russia only a year, but he remained in St. Petersburg for the rest of his life—more than sixty years. At first he was a dancer, and he also restaged some of the Romantic ballets he had learned in France. Then he began to create his own ballets. He became chief choreographer of the Russian Imperial Ballet in 1862, and started to choreograph one ballet after another. By the end of his life he had made more than sixty full-length ballets. Today we still applaud his creations, especially *The Sleeping Beauty* and *Swan Lake*. It is largely Petipa's contributions that made Russian ballet the most successful in the world.

Russian Ballerinas, Imported and Native

Though the language of the ballet continued to be French, in the second half of the nineteenth century the center of the dancing world moved from Paris to St. Petersburg (now Leningrad), then the capital of Imperial Russia. The kick was still called *battement*, and the turn *pirouette*, but the best dancers from all over the world were going to Russia to perform. Two Italian ballerinas who came to Russia, Virginia Zucchi (in 1885) and Pierina Legnani (in 1893), were probably the very best of their time. Zucchi was a great dramatic ballerina, and Legnani was noted for her technique.

Pierina Legnani, caricatured above right, and Virginia Zucchi, left, were Italian ballerinas who became very popular and influential in Russia in the 1890s. Artists not only made beautiful pictures of ballerinas as we have seen on earlier pages but also enjoyed making caricatures of them. The caricature of Legnani is by Nicholas Legat, a Russian dancer and teacher.

She could execute the most difficult steps perfectly. As the Black Swan in *Swan Lake* (1895), Legnani was the first ballerina to do thirty-two *fouettés* (turns done on one foot while the other leg whips the dancer into moving like a top).

Legnani was the first ballerina to dance the double part of Odette, the gentle Queen of the Swans, and Odile, the evil Black Swan, in *Swan Lake*. The ballet was choreographed by Marius Petipa and Lev Ivanov; the music was by the famous Russian composer Tchaikovsky.

Zucchi and Legnani could do steps on *pointe* that Taglioni could not do. Ballerinas had experimented with their shoes since Taglioni's time, and the little bit of darning she had added to her shoes had evolved into a stiff, hard toe shoe with the *pointe* almost flat. This enabled the ballerina to balance longer on *pointe* and to do difficult steps such as *pirouettes* and *fouettés* on the tips of her toes. Zucchi and Legnani helped to bring about this new development in ballet technique.

In time the Russian ballet, under the direction of Petipa and with his and Ivanov's choreography, became the greatest ballet in the world. Eventually Petipa no longer had to invite foreign ballerinas to dance in his great ballet spectacles. His own Russian dancers became just as good as those from other countries. Two are particularly important. They are Olga Preobrajenska and Mathilde Kchessinska. Kchessinska was able to do the famous thirty-two *fouettés* and was the only *prima ballerina assoluta* in the history of Russia.

Fokine and Diaghilev

Fashions in ballet, like fashions in clothes, change. We have seen how these changes took place from the time of Lafontaine to Camargo, from Sallé to Taglioni, and from Elssler to Legnani. In choreography ballet developed from Noverre to Perrot to Petipa. Petipa grew old, and there were many young choreographers and dancers who were tired of his ballets. They had their own ideas and wanted to try something new. One of these was a young dancer-choreographer named Michel Fokine.

When Fokine began to choreograph shortly after 1900, he started to change things around. Before him, most choreographers, when they were making story-ballets about Egypt or Greece or India or other lands, used exactly the same steps that they used in other ballets. They changed the costumes but not the movements! Fokine's ballets, however, tried to make both movements and costumes partly authentic. So when Fokine made an Oriental ballet, he used the rippling arms

Russian ballerinas of worldwide fame came along right after such Italians as Zucchi and Legnani had visited Russia. Two of these were Olga Preobrajenska (above) and Mathilde Kchessinska (below). "Preo," as the first was nicknamed, taught ballet in Paris until she died at 91. Kchessinska married a grand duke and was given the title "Her Serene Highness." She will be one hundred years old in 1972!

and the hip-sways of the East. Or when he created his warriors' dance in *Prince Igor*, he combined certain exciting ballet steps with the whirling movements, the bow-and-arrow aiming and shooting of wild Tartar tribesmen.

Fokine was not popular with the older people who managed the Russian Imperial Ballet; but he fascinated one Russian who could neither dance nor choreograph nor teach—the producer Sergei Diaghilev.

In 1909, Diaghilev took a company of young Russian dancers from the Imperial Ballet, along with new repertoire by Fokine, to Paris. The French, who had been bored with ballet since the romantic ballets of magic had faded, became very excited about Diaghilev's new company— which they called *Les Ballets Russes*, "The Russian Ballets."

From that time on, for twenty years, until he died in 1929, Diaghilev excited Europe and even America with Fokine's ballets: *Firebird, Petrouchka, Les Sylphides* (a ballet that paid tribute to the old *La Sylphide*), and the wild dances from *Prince Igor*. He also did ballets by another Russian, Leonide Massine, and by the young George Balanchine.

When Diaghilev took ballet out of Russia and gave it to the world with the *Ballet Russe*, he completed something that Mademoiselle Subligny had begun more than two hundred years before when she took ballet from Paris to London—he made ballet international. Some of his important young stars were Vaslav Nijinsky, Tamara Karsavina, and Anna Pavlova.

Anna Pavlova

In the early part of this century, Anna Pavlova was the most famous ballerina in the world. The ballet solo of *The Dying Swan* was made especially for her by Michel Fokine. Pavlova danced the part all over the world. She came to America for the first time in 1910, and she came back again and again until her death in 1931.

America had lost interest in ballet until Pavlova danced and reminded them how beautiful and exciting it could be. With her came a renewed interest in the ballet. Pavlova, of course, danced more than *The Dying Swan*. She also danced in *Giselle* and was Princess Aurora in Petipa's *The Sleeping Beauty* and the mischievous Swanilda in *Coppelia*. She eventually formed a ballet company of her own and had choreographers make ballets just for her. In her time, and especially in America, she was ballet itself, and *The Dying Swan* was Pavlova's special mark.

Anna Pavlova, the world's most famous ballerina, in performance and in her dressing room on tour.

Tamara Karsavina, a *prima ballerina*, and one of the greatest men dancers of all time, Vaslav Nijinsky.

Tamara Karsavina

Tamara Karsavina was one of the major dancers who left the Russian Imperial Ballet in 1909 to dance with Sergei Diaghilev's *Ballets Russes* in Paris. She was almost the same age as Pavlova, and though she never enjoyed the worldwide popularity that Pavlova did, she became the *prima ballerina* of the *Ballets Russes*. Balletomanes—people who are ballet "fans"—were divided in their loyalties to the two dancers, with many saying that Karsavina was the better dancer. Her favorite partner was Vaslav Nijinsky, the greatest male dancer of his time.

The ballet belongs as much to the male dancer as to the ballerina, though there have been times when the girls have outshone the gentlemen—such as when the ballerinas began to dance on *pointe*. Before Camargo's time, though, when the ballerinas wore long heavy dresses, the men could do much more exciting steps. And even after Camargo, Gaetan Vestris and his son Auguste Vestris were great stars of ballet. The ballerina was called "Queen of the Dance," but Auguste was called "God of the Dance."

Vaslav Nijinsky

Vaslav Nijinsky too was a dancing god. He could jump higher than was thought possible and did fantastic leaps, turns, twists, runs, and falls that most athletes could not do. His performances were more than athletic feats. Nijinsky was a great artist. He was the spirit of a rose in *Spectre de la Rose*; he was a flashing warrior in *Prince Igor*. He played the sad puppet with the heart of a man in *Petrouchka*; and he was a magical creature of the woods in a ballet he himself choreographed, *Afternoon of a Faun*.

Another "Russian"—Markova

During the reigns of Petipa and Diaghilev the ballet had become so Russian that it seemed you almost had to be Russian in order to be a ballerina. Then a little English girl, Lilian Alicia Marks, showed such talent in her dancing that she was called "the miniature Pavlova." When she was only fourteen, the great Diaghilev engaged her to dance in the *Ballets Russes*. He also changed her name to Alicia Markova. She became the first world-famous English ballerina in this century. She was the *prima ballerina* of the Sadler's Wells Ballet (which Queen Elizabeth II renamed the Royal Ballet), and she also danced with the American ballet companies for many years until she retired to become director of ballet at the Metropolitan Opera House in New York City. She and her

Alicia Markova, England's first important ballerina of this century.

partner, Anton Dolin (an Englishman who was born Patrick Healey-Kay), had their own company, and the Markova-Dolin Ballet traveled all over the world. Markova was most famous for her *Giselle*, but she danced all the classical roles. Her *Dying Swan* was also famous, which is to be expected—she *had* been called "the miniature Pavlova."

Danilova and the Ballets Russes de Monte Carlo

During the 1930s, the 1940s, and into the 1950s, Markova shared the spotlight with Alexandra Danilova. Like earlier rivals—Camargo and Sallé, Taglioni and Elssler, Zucchi and Legnani, Kchessinska and Preobrajenska, Pavlova and Karsavina—Markova and Danilova each had their special fans. They were rivals on stage, good friends off stage.

Markova was tiny, delicate, and shy. Danilova was like bubbles of ginger ale, full of pep and energy. Both were dancers with Diaghilev's *Ballets Russes*, but the older Danilova was a star when the teen-age Markova was a beginner. When Markova went to London after Diaghilev's death in 1929, Danilova became the ballerina of a company called the *Ballets Russes de Monte Carlo*, which was very popular. In addition to Danilova (and sometimes Markova) the company arrived with three talented teen-agers who were affectionately called "Baby Ballerinas." They were Tamara Toumanova, Irina Baronova, and Tatiana Riabouchinska.

One of Danilova's most popular parts was that of the mischievous Swanilda in *Coppélia*, and the audiences loved her as the sparkling Street Dancer in *Le Beau Danube* and as the Glove Seller in *Gaîté Parisienne*. Her fans began calling her *prima ballerina assoluta*, since there was no longer a Czar in Russia to give her the title. She became an American citizen, and when she retired she taught and staged some of the great classical ballets, such as *The Nutcracker*. To her pupils she is known with respect and affection as "Madame D."

There were excellent *premiers danseurs* too with the *Ballets Russes de Monte Carlo* of Danilova's time. Frederic Franklin from England was one of her favorite partners. André Eglevsky was born in Moscow and studied in Paris with Kchessinska, dancing the Prince in *Swan Lake* when he was fifteen. He was especially famous for his elevation—that is, his ability to jump very high, giving the illusion of resting in the air. Another *premier danseur* with the company, Igor Youskevitch, did not start to study ballet until he was grown. He was a fine athlete first and then became a dancer. He was famous for his technique and for his ability to "partner"—to lift, catch and support the ballerina. This made him a favorite partner for most ballerinas.

The lady of the perfect legs, Alexandra Danilova.

Baby Ballerinas: Tamara Toumanova (left), Irina Baronova in the movie *Florian* (center), and Tatiana Riabouchinska with her husband, David Lichine, in *Graduation Ball* (right).

COURTESY S. HUROK

COURTESY S. HUROK

Left top and bottom, Galina Ulanova, once prima ballerina of the Bolshoi Ballet and now one of the most famous teachers in the Soviet Union. In the upper picture she instructs the young Ekaterina Maximova, and in the lower she appears as New York saw her on the stage of the old Metropolitan Opera House as Juliet in the ballet of *Romeo and Juliet*. *Above*, the Bolshoi *corps de ballet* in *La Bayadère. Facing page*, Maya Plisetskaya, now *primà ballerina* of the Bolshoi, is Odile, the Black Swan, in *Swan Lake*.

Russian Ballet Today

When Diaghilev took his *Ballets Russes* to the West, he did not take *all* of Russian ballet with him. In 1917, with the Russian Revolution, the great Imperial Ballets became State Ballets of the Soviet Union. In Leningrad (once St. Petersburg), Moscow, and in other big cities, the companies continued to perform, and lavishly, their great classics, *The Sleeping Beauty, Swan Lake, The Nutcracker, Bayaderka, Don Quixote*, and dozens and dozens more. New choreographers came along to make new ballets, some of them quite classical, like *Cinderella* or *Romeo and Juliet*, and others more modern but not so modern as American ballets can be. Great ballet stars of this later age have gained worldwide fame—Ulanova, Plisetskaya, Maximova, Soloviev, Sizova, Vasiliev, and many more—and the huge national ballet schools in Russia are still envied by dancers all over the world, by dancers who would like to study where Pavlova, Nijinsky, Karsavina, Fokine, Danilova, and Balanchine once had dance lessons.

Harriet Hoctor, ballet star in Broadway shows.

Nana Gollner in the Mad Scene from *Giselle*.

American Ballet in the Twentieth Century

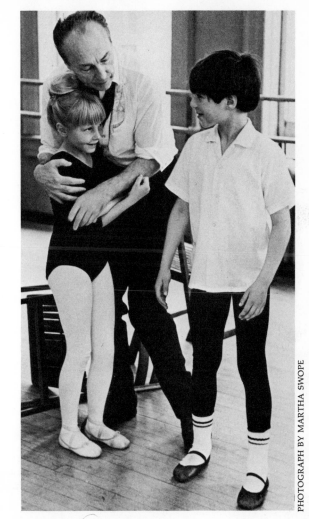

Before 1930 there were no big American ballet companies. American girls who wanted to be ballerinas could do so only in an opera, an operetta, a musical comedy, vaudeville, or a revue. But if those dancers were starting out today, some of them would be in ballet companies. Marilyn Miller, a *pointe* dancer who starred in Broadway musicals, is said to have been the most respected star on stage in America at the time. Maria Gambarelli, Patricia Bowman, and Harriet Hoctor were other Broadway ballerinas. "Gamby," as Gambarella was nicknamed, also appeared in recitals, and Bowman appeared in ballet productions by Fokine, but the three were most often to be found in motion pictures or on the stages of motion-picture theaters—or elsewhere in "show biz."

But after 1930, America began to make itself important in international ballet. George Balanchine came from Europe to direct the School of American Ballet as well as a company which was to grow into the New York City Ballet. And in 1939, the American Ballet Theatre, now one of the greatest companies in the world, was founded.

One great American dancer was Nana Gollner—the first American girl in this century to become a *prima ballerina* with a European ballet company. As a young girl she had been partly paralyzed by polio, and her doctor recommended dancing lessons to strengthen her muscles. Nana studied so hard that not only did she recover completely, but her feet became so strong that she could stand on *pointe* in her bare feet. In America she was best known as the *prima ballerina* of the American Ballet Theatre.

The age of the American ballerina, which began with Nana Gollner, continued with many other American girls who studied hard and worked their way up from *corps de ballet* through soloist rank to ballerina. One such dancer was born Nora Koreff in New York City. At one time she changed her name to Nura Kureva, to sound Russian. When she realized she could be American and a ballerina too, then she made herself Nora Kaye. She was very good in the old classical ballets, but she was particularly successful in very modern, highly dramatic ballets.

George Balanchine, artistic director and chief choreographer for the New York City Ballet, rehearses child dancers.

Today's dramatic ballets do not separate dance steps from pantomime. Instead, modern choreographers combine steps with gestures in a single movement. In the old classical ballets, a dancer might execute, on *pointe*, a turn in *arabesque* because it is exciting to look at and pretty. In a modern ballet, she might play the part of a girl who cannot make up her mind, and so while her mind is spinning, the ballerina's body spins too, suggesting on the *outside* what is happening *inside* of her. After performing *Pillar of Fire* by the great English choreographer Antony Tudor, Nora Kaye stood on the stage of the old Metropolitan Opera House in New York through twenty-seven curtain calls while the audience cheered her and Tudor and his ballet!

Ballet is not always serious. Sometimes it can be very funny. Janet Reed, very tiny and very sweet, was always good at comedy. In *Filling Station*, she played the part of a rich girl whose boy friend had let her drink too much wine; so when the ballerina moved on *pointe*, you could not be sure just where she was going, and just as she would be about to fall down, someone would catch her. In *Con Amore*, she was a lady with three beaux: a rich man, a sailor, and a scholar. They all arrived to call on her at the same time, or almost, and it was fun watching her try to hide them from each other. In the ballet version of Shakespeare's *A Midsummer Night's Dream* there is much humor, most of it started by Puck, the impish fairy, who scurries around getting everyone into trouble and out again.

Two American Ballet Theatre productions: *far left*, a dramatic ballet, Antony Tudor's *Pillar of Fire* with Nora Kaye and Hugh Laing; *near left*, a comedy-jazz ballet, Jerome Robbins's *Interplay*, with Janet Reed and John Kriza.

2. A Gallery of Modern Stars

Maria Tallchief

Indians on Toe

You cannot be much more American than an American Indian, and you will not find a much more Indian name than Tall Chief. Both Maria and Marjorie Tallchief (the two words were made into one) were born on an Osage Indian reservation in Oklahoma. Maria, although she toured all over the world and danced in Russia itself, had her career mainly in America. She danced in the great classics—*Swan Lake, The Nutcracker, grand pas de deux* from *Don Quixote*—but she was most famous for her brilliant dancing in ballets that were made especially for her by the great choreographer, George Balanchine, artistic director of the New York City Ballet. These were almost all one-act ballets using classical dance technique but no story—beautiful dancing for the sake of beautiful movement. Maria was the first American ballerina to be guest artist at the Paris Opéra since Augusta Maywood danced there one hundred years before. She was also the first American ballerina to dance with the old Royal Danish Ballet. Marjorie, although she danced with such American companies as the American Ballet Theatre and the Harkness Ballet, spent most of her career in Europe. She became the *prima ballerina* of the Paris Opéra Ballet. Certainly, she was the first American Indian to have that job. So she learned to speak French; and her husband, the dancer-choreographer George Skibine, learned to speak Osage.

Marjorie Tallchief   Rosella Hightower (with Erik Bruhn)   Yvonne Chouteau

A Cuban Ballerina—Alicia Alonso

Alicia Alonso is the most famous Latin American ballerina in the world and indeed she has danced all over the world, from New York to Paris, from Moscow to Peking. She was born and brought up in Cuba; and Cuba is her home now, where she heads Cuba's National Ballet. But almost all of her ballet training was in the United States. She danced in Broadway musicals and then joined the American Ballet Theatre in 1940. She too came all the way up from *corps de ballet* through demisoloist and soloist to ballerina and *prima ballerina*. Although she was Cuban, on her first visit to Russia, where she was a guest star with Soviet companies, she was the first American-trained ballerina to be seen in Russia. She succeeded Markova as the greatest *Giselle* of her time; and she also danced in many other classics, such as *Swan Lake*, *The Nutcracker*, and *Coppélia*. She was, and is, equally successful in modern dramatic ballets by Agnes de Mille and Antony Tudor.

Dame Margot

Margot Fonteyn, *prima ballerina* of England's Royal Ballet, not only plays a queen in *Swan Lake* and a princess in *The Sleeping Beauty*, but also she has a real title. In honor of her beautiful dancing, Queen Elizabeth II of England gave her the title "Dame of the British Empire." Dame Margot was the first British ballerina to study all the courses at the Sadler's Wells Ballet School (now the Royal Ballet School). While still very young she danced important roles, and when Markova left to dance with other companies, then Fonteyn became the *prima ballerina*. One of her most famous roles is Princess Aurora and another is the double part of Odette and Odile, but some very beautiful ballets have been made especially for her by Sir Frederick Ashton, one of the world's finest choreographers. He did the three-act *Ondine* and the three-act *Sylvia* especially for her. He has also choreographed ballets not only for her but also for her and a dancer who was her favorite partner for several years, the Russian star, Rudolf Nureyev. Dame Margot became the most popular ballerina in the world.

Alicia Alonso, Cuban-born, U.S.-trained, and now Cuba's most famous star, as Odette, the Swan Queen, in *Swan Lake*.

Facing page, the *pas de deux* from *Black Swan* with Dame Margot Fonteyn as Odile and Richard Cragun, American *premier danseur* of the Stuttgart Ballet, as her partner. Here they are photographed on stage in Boston.

Nathalie Krassovksa, with Leon Danielian.

"Tata"

One of the prettiest of the senior ballerinas is Nathalie Krassovska. Her real last name is Leslie. Her father was Scottish and her mother was Russian, but she took her mother's family name, Krassovska, because it was an important name in ballet in Russia. "Tata," as she is called, is not only very beautiful but she also has a fine classical technique. She does gentle dances, like *The Dying Swan* or *Les Sylphides* (she was a pupil of Fokine), but she can also do such very difficult *grand pas deux* as *Black Swan* or *Don Quixote*, with their *fouettés*, *pirouettes*, and long balances on one *pointe*.

"Brigitta"

Vera Zorina is very beautiful here as Persephone. She was born Eva Brigitta Hartwig (her parents were Norwegian), and she became well known in Europe as "Brigitta." When she was asked to be guest star with the *Ballets Russes de Monte Carlo*, the director insisted that she have a Russian name, and gave her the choice of a long list of Russian names. The only one she could pronounce was the very last name on the list, Vera Zorina, so she took it. As Zorina, she became an important ballet dancer; but more than that, she became a dancing star in musical comedies on Broadway and in motion pictures. George Balanchine, who has made dances for many ballerinas, did much choreography especially for Zorina. Today, she does mostly acting, but because she has always been a dancer, she still moves with great beauty in whatever roles she plays.

Tanaquil LeClercq

Tanaquil LeClercq was another young dancer whom Balanchine helped to become a ballerina. She was quite tall and very thin, so "Mr. B." (as he is known in the world of ballet) made some ballets which showed off her long legs, her high kicks, and her ability to do angular steps attractively. Here she is with Jerome Robbins in Mr. B.'s *Bourrée Fantasque*.

Far left, Vera Zorina, actress-dancer and former ballerina, in Stravinsky's danced-opera *Persephone*. *Center and above*, Jerome Robbins, shown with Tanaquil LeClercq in Balanchine's *Bourrée Fantasque* and conducting a rehearsal.

39

"Millie"

Her friends call her "Millie," but on stage she is the glamorous Melissa Hayden, ballerina. She is Canadian, and although she dances in Canada once in a while, her career is in the United States, where she is a ballerina with the New York City Ballet. She has also danced with the American Ballet Theatre and other companies. There is no role too difficult for her to do. She has excelled in the great classics, such as *Swan Lake*, and she has been a big success in very modern ballets—many of them choreographed by Balanchine and some of them made just for her. In *Agon*, for example, she does some steps that were never seen in ballet before. In the ballet of *A Midsummer Night's Dream*, she dances the part of a queen, Titania, the queen of fairyland. Here, her dancing is really classical ballet, but in a ballet called *Illuminations*, she dances with one foot in a toe shoe and the other bare.

A Batch of Ballerinas

The New York City Ballet seems to turn out ballerinas, or at the very least skillful young soloists, as swiftly as spring brings May flowers. For a good many years, Maria Tallchief was the *prima ballerina*; Melissa Hayden and Patricia Wilde, with her high leaps, came from other companies to become longtime members. Later there were the delicate, shy (she even seems like a flower) Mimi Paul (who comes from Washington, D.C.), and Suzanne Farrell, for whom Balanchine made new and exciting ballets. Diana Adams, who does not dance any more, was a very beautiful ballerina; and the great French ballerina, Violette Verdy, who does dance, is a very great artist in her adopted company. Allegra Kent was another dancer who moved from the *corps* to ballerina rank in the New York City Ballet. There are also two "Pats," Patricia McBride who is the favorite partner of Edward Villella, and Patricia Neary, who has red hair, long legs, and can kick the back of her head. Very often the New York City Ballet does not list its dancers on billboards or in advertisements, and it does not call anyone a ballerina—just "principal." So you have to look carefully and make your own decision about who is a ballerina and who is not.

Left, Melissa Hayden, the girl-warrior in *The Duel. Facing page,* Patricia Wilde and Paul Sutherland, dancing on the promenade of Lincoln Center's Philharmonic Hall.

Above, Patricia McBride and Nicholas Magallanes in Balanchine's very modern *Episodes. Right,* Diana Adams and Arthur Mitchell in the Balanchine-Stravinsky *Agon,* a new ballet based on old forms. *Facing page,* Violette Verdy dances in the first theater ever built for dance, Jacob's Pillow at Lee, Massachusetts.

Left, Jacques d'Amboise, star of the New York City Ballet. *Above*, Edward Villella, principal of the New York City Ballet and a ballet favorite with regional ballets and TV. *Facing page*, the finale of Jerome Robbins's ballet to Stravinsky's *Les Noces*, American Ballet Theatre. The paintings are by Oliver Smith, co-director with Lucia Chase of the American Ballet Theatre.

Two Premiers Danseurs

The New York City Ballet also produces some fine male dancers. Two of the very best—and they are among the best male dancers in the world—are Jacques d'Amboise and Edward Villella. Both of them actually grew up in this company, and both of them are special favorites of New York City Ballet audiences. Jacques is tall and Eddie is short, but both are brilliant classical dancers; both leap very high and turn very fast. But of course they move differently, just as different people speak the same language but do it just a little differently—high or low, soft or loud, fast or slow, with a Southern accent or a New England one. Naturally, there should be only one *premier danseur* (just as there is only one *prima ballerina*) to a company, but it is difficult to say whether Jacques or Eddie is the *premier danseur* of the New York City Ballet. However, since the New York City Ballet does not call anyone a *premier danseur*, you can decide for yourself who should have the title. Maybe both?

The Queen's Own Dancers

Great Britain's Royal Ballet has as its extra special patroness the Queen herself, Elizabeth II. Officially this is her company, and she numbers among her Royal Dancers not only the fabulous Dame Margot Fonteyn but also Svetlana Beriosova (you might think that she would be a Russian ballerina but she grew up in America and studied ballet here); blond Antoinette Sibley, who dances Titania, Queen of Fairyland, in the British ballet, *The Dream* (taken from "A Midsummer Night's Dream"), choreographed by Sir Frederick Ashton, in which her partner, Anthony Dowell, plays the King of Fairyland, Oberon (the American Oberon is Edward Villella); Merle Park, who often dances with the famous Russian star Rudolf Nureyev. The Royal Ballet also boasts some fine male dancers. Nureyev is a guest star with the Royal troupe and there are the versatile Tony Dowell; Alexander Grant, who is a great clown and loves to do comedy parts; David Blair, once a very elegant *danseur* (now retired) and also an expert at teaching whole ballet companies how to dance *Swan Lake, Giselle,* and the other great ballets of long ago; and, of course, Sir Fred himself—who was the director of the Royal Ballet until 1970, and its leading choreographer (he has made more than forty ballets!) and also was a dancer (he played one of the Ugly Sisters, a very ugly one, in *Cinderella*).

Facing page, Svetlana Beriosova, with Keith Rosson, in Fokine's *Les Sylphides.*   *Left,* Nadia Nerina and David Blair in *Swan Lake*.

Sir Frederick Ashton is not only England's greatest choreographer, he is also a great comic performer. On this page he is shown as one of the Ugly Sisters in his own ballet *Cinderella*. One of Sir Frederick's choreographic masterpieces is *The Dream*, based on Shakespeare's play *A Midsummer Night's Dream*, and on the next page Antoinette Sibley and Anthony Dowell are shown as Titania and Oberon, the king of the fairies. (The character Bottom, with a donkey's head, is Alexander Grant.)

The Danes not only boast of the oldest kingdom in Europe but also the oldest royal ballet. Here, in one of their palaces, the present royal family is dressed to attend a gala performance of the ballet: King Frederik IX, center, and, left to right, Princess Benedikte, Princess Anne-Marie (now the Queen of Greece), Queen Ingrid of Denmark, and Crown Princess Margrethe, who will one day rule Denmark.

The King's Own Dancers

The Kings of Denmark have been patrons of the ballet for more than two hundred years. The present king, Frederik IX, actually took ballet lessons when he was a young Prince. He is a fine musician, and very often when he goes to the ballet and sits on a special throne in the royal box at the Royal Theater in the Royal Square in Copenhagen, he has a musical score in his lap for *Napoli* (his favorite ballet, choreographed by Auguste Bournonville, who made many Danish dance masterpieces) or *Coppélia*, or some other ballet classic. King Frederik, whose ancestors have ruled Denmark from the days of Gorm the Old and Harald Bluetooth of a thousand years ago, takes special delight in his Royal Dancers. Among them are Margrethe Schanne, most famous for the title role of *La Sylphide* in the same ballet that an earlier Dane, Lucile Grahn, first danced in Denmark; the blond and beautiful Kirsten Simone, who puts on a black wig to be the Spanish *Carmen*; Fredbjørn Bjørnsson, who has been able to change, as he has grown older, from a bounding Dane with great leaps and fast turns to one of the best character-dancers, really an actor-dancer, that you will ever see; Henning Kronstam, a *premier danseur* who can play everything from the Prince in *Swan Lake* and the Poet in *La Sonnambula* to Balanchine's *Apollo* and a mad old man in *The Lesson*. And, of course, a Dane who is the greatest *premier danseur noble* (and that is a very special title, as you can see) of our time, Erik Bruhn.

The Royal Danish Ballet. *Below*, Kirsten Simone and Flemming Flindt in Roland Petit's ballet of the opera *Carmen*. *Right*, Niels Kehlet.

PHOTOGRAPH BY VON HAVEN PRESSE

More photographs of the Royal Danish Ballet. *Left*, Margrethe Schanne is sketched in a leap; the drawing was used as a postage stamp in Denmark. *Below*, Niels Kehlet as the sorcerer in a ballet about a Lapland myth, *The Moon Reindeer*. *Facing page*, Kirsten Simone and Henning Kronstam in Ashton's *Romeo and Juliet*.

Above, Toni Lander as the Moon Reindeer and Bruce Marks as the hero in the American Ballet Theatre's production of the Danish-Lapp ballet. *Right,* Italy's Carla Fracci and Denmark's Erik Bruhn in *Giselle.*

54

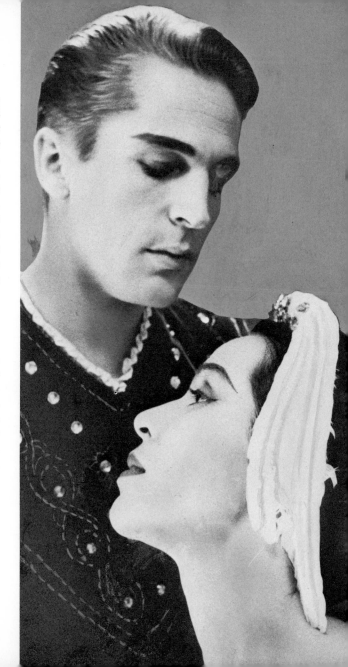

Toni and Bruce

Toni Lander and Bruce Marks are husband and wife. Toni was born and brought up in Denmark, where she was an important dancer with the Royal Danish Ballet. Bruce is a New Yorker, and he had his dance training in modern dance, which is quite different from classical ballet. He made his début when he was ten as a child dancer in a modern dance work called *Rites*. Then he went to New York City's High School of the Performing Arts, where he began to take ballet lessons. Eventually, Bruce turned into a ballet dancer, and Toni, a great European star, came to America. They met when they joined the American Ballet Theatre, and they dance together almost all the time. In *Swan Lake*, Toni is the Queen of the Swans and the evil Odile, and Bruce is the Prince. But they are just as fine in modern ballets, such as the very dramatic *Miss Julie*, by the Swedish choreographer Birgit Cullberg, as they are in the classical *Etudes* by the Danish Harald Lander. In fact, *Etudes* is very much like a marvelous ballet class which starts with a simple *plié* and all the exercises at the ballet *barre*, and goes through all kinds of *pirouettes* and *fouettés* to *grands jetés* and *tours en l'air*. Toni and Bruce are often its stars, with the whole company dancing, *Etudes* is something like an exciting game of follow-the-leader through ballet!

Erik Bruhn

Erik Bruhn is the most famous Danish *premier danseur* in the world. He is blond, very handsome, and very elegant in classical and romantic roles. And because he is elegant and princely as well as having the best male ballet technique you will see anywhere, he is called a *premier danseur noble*. Erik not only dances with his own Royal Danish Ballet but also with the American Ballet Theatre, and very often he makes guest appearances with other world companies. Erik is very versatile. He can do many different and difficult parts. Of course he is a splendid Prince Siegfried in *Swan Lake* and Count Albrecht in *Giselle*, and a dashing figure in the *grand pas de deux* from *Don Quixote*, but he is also a very odd butler in *Miss Julie* and a very romantic young man in *Carmen* (in which he wears a black wig!). He is also very good in the old Danish ballets by Bournonville, especially in the famous *La Sylphide* that the Danish Lucile Grahn first danced more than a century ago. Erik, of course, could not dance with Grahn, but he has danced with the great ballerinas of his time: Markova, Maria Tallchief, Marjorie Tallchief, Nora Kaye, Rosella Hightower, Svetlana

Maria Tallchief and Erik Bruhn in the New York City Ballet's one-act *Swan Lake*.

PHOTOGRAPH BY JACK MITCHELL

Beriosova, Violette Verdy, Sonia Arova, the famous French ballerina Yvette Chauviré, the American Ballet Theatre's ballerina Lupe Serrano, and of course all the Danish ballerinas, such as Toni Lander, Kirsten Simone, and Anna Laerkesen, and Italy's greatest dancer, Carla Fracci.

When Erik danced at the Royal Opera House in London, his fans in the boxes and balconies showered him with rose petals as he bowed at the end of a performance. He looked every inch like "Prince Erik," *premier danseur noble.*

Rudi Nureyev

Rudi Nureyev made the biggest jump ever done by a dancer. He was in Paris with the Kirov Ballet from Leningrad when he was ordered by Russian officials to go back to Russia by himself. He did not want to go, so at the Paris airport, he jumped away from his Russian guards and ran and leaped into the arms of the French police. This "leap to freedom" was approved by the French government, and Rudolf Nureyev—who had been born in Siberia—belonged to the world. Rudi moves with the grace of a cat and has a remarkable ballet technique. He wears his hair quite long and the expression on his face is very solemn and mysterious, except when he smiles; and then he looks like a little boy. Like Erik Bruhn, he is a fine artist of the theater as well as a *virtuoso*. You will find him as a Count in *Giselle*, a Prince in *Swan Lake*, Romeo in *Romeo and Juliet*; and in a crazy modern ballet, he runs fast in a circle around the stage and up and down a staircase and then dives headfirst right through a huge pair of painted lips which make the scene for the stage! Rudi of course has danced with many ballerinas, first those in his native country at the Kirov and later with European ballerinas of the West. The most famous of these was Dame Margot Fonteyn. Whenever they dance together, audiences sigh happily, applaud loud and long at the end of the performance, and toss flowers at their feet as they stand before the curtains to bow. Rudi, like Erik, likes to do choreography as well as to dance. You would think they might be rivals. They are not. Rudi and Erik are the best of friends.

Facing page, Yuri Vladimirov soars high in the Bolshoi Ballet's *Rite of Spring*.

Rudolf Nureyev in a classical leap.

PHOTOGRAPH BY RON PROTAS

"The Wonder of the World"—Ulanova

Galina Ulanova (Oo-LAHN-ova) recently stopped dancing, but she was the most famous Russian dancer of modern times. She danced, of course, in *Swan Lake*; she made you cry when she acted the Mad Scene in *Giselle*, and as Juliet, in the Russian ballet version of *Romeo and Juliet*, although she was fifty years old when American audiences first saw her, she looked and danced like an innocent girl of fourteen! As the *prima ballerina* of the Bolshoi Ballet (*Bolshoi* means "big" in Russian) of Moscow, she also danced in ballets at home that we have never seen, such as *Fountains of Bakhchisarai*. You can see her every once in a while in Russian movies she made while she was Russia's foremost dancer, and I am quite sure that as you watch her dance, you will know why someone called her "The Wonder of the World."

Marvelous Maya and Other Russians

When Ulanova retired from the stage in order to teach ballet to children and to help talented young Russian girls to develop into ballerinas, the position of *prima ballerina* of the Bolshoi Ballet came to an exciting dancer who had already made American dance fans sit on the edges of their seats, Maya Plisetskaya (Plee-SETS-kaya). Ulanova was a very gentle dancer with a rather sad expression or an innocent one. Maya flashes smiles that dazzle you. She moves like a whirlwind, and she has so much energy you think she just might explode. When she does *grands jetés*, her back leg nearly touches the back of her head. Naturally, she dances Odette-Odile in *Swan Lake*; but she is also like a firecracker in the full-length *Don Quixote*; and just to surprise you, she dances *The Dying Swan* so softly, with wonderful rippling arms, that you think you are looking at a fluttering bird.

The Bolshoi Ballet's Maya Plisetskaya is famous both for her leaps and for her back kick. On the facing page she combines the two in *Don Quixote*.

Lupe Serrano and Royes Fernandez, although they are not married to each other, are almost as much of a team in the American Ballet Theatre as Toni Lander and Bruce Marks. From their names, you might think that they are both Spanish, and you would be partly right. Lupe was born in distant Chile but grew up in Mexico, being actually Mexican; but Royes was born in our own New Orleans. His ancestors were both Spanish and French. Lupe is mostly a classical ballerina, and when she went to Russia with the American Ballet Theatre, Russian audiences cheered her more loudly than any other American ballerina. She can do modern ballets, but she is happiest in *Swan Lake, Giselle,* or as the mischievous girl in one of the oldest ballets in the world, *La Fille Mal Gardée*—"The Badly Guarded Daughter." Royes usually dances with her in *Fille,* playing an equally mischievous boy; but he also dances the roles of Princes, Counts, and Nobles and is, like Bruhn, called a *danseur noble.*

Another ballerina in the Ballet Theatre is Eleanor d'Antuono, who dances in classical ballets with Gayle Young. John Kriza, who has just retired as a dancer, danced for thirty-five years about every part you could name from *Billy the Kid* through the jazzy *Fancy Free* and *Interplay* (by Jerome Robbins) to really extreme ballets like Herbert Ross's *Caprichos,* in which he did a dance with a girl (Ruth Ann Koesun) limp as a rag doll that he tossed all over the place. Johnny could really do anything. So can Scott Douglas (until recently with his company) from Texas, and all know this to be true because Scott can be an elegant Cavalier (almost a Prince) in one ballet and a modern dancer in the next. But then the dancers in the American Ballet Theatre are expected to do everything well, cowboy or jazz, modern dance or folk dance, dramatic dance or the purest classical ballet.

Facing page, Lupe Serrano as a peasant girl (Giselle) and Royes Fernandez as a prince in disguise in Act I of *Giselle. Right,* a real American ballet with cowboys and cowgirls—*Rodeo,* a folk ballet by Agnes de Mille. Here it is danced by the American Ballet Theatre.

Newcomers in American Ballet

There are more ballet troupes in America today than ever before and you will find these companies from coast to coast. Some, of course, like the Atlanta Ballet and the San Francisco Ballet, have been around for a long time. Others are quite new, and some are brand new. Robert Joffrey, the choreographer, has headed a series of companies but today he is the director of the City Center Joffrey Ballet which is the resident ballet company at the New York City Center. The Harkness Ballet, which gained international fame for its brilliant dancers and its imaginative ballets (new works, both classical in technique and modern dance) from 1964 to 1970 continued with the Harkness Youth Dancers. In 1968, Eliot Feld, a fine dancer and an exciting young choreographer with the American Ballet Theatre, left to form his own group, the American Ballet Company, which quickly became still another important addition to the growing list of American dance enterprises.

The dancers? Some wonderful newcomers have arrived to grace our ballet stages. Ballet fans, attending performances by these and the older companies, look at these newcomers and pick their favorites. Lone Isaksen from Denmark, Helgi Thomasson from Iceland, Yoko Morishita from Japan, or Lawrence Rhodes, Brunilda Ruiz, Susan Magno, Christine Sarry, Ted Kivitt, Ivan Nagy (who came to us from Hungary), Elizabeth Carroll, Paul Sutherland, Richard Cragun (an American who become a star with Germany's Stuttgart Ballet) and more, more, more!

In ballet, everyone waits for the appearance of a new ballerina, a new star. It is not that we do not love the ballerinas already with us, but the ballet must think about tomorrow as well as today. Camargo, Taglioni, Pavlova have all gone. Ulanova, Danilova, Markova no longer dance. Fonteyn will retire soon and so will others we worship today. The younger ballerinas are hoping to be *prima ballerinas*, and the soloists want to be ballerinas, and the students want to be ballet dancers. So we look around us and try to spot, to pick out, the next big star. Maybe one will be Suzanne Farrell, formerly of the New York City Ballet. Perhaps one of the great ones will be Cynthia Gregory of the Ballet Theatre, who jumped from *corps de ballet* to ballerina in one year. She has already been a big success in the full-length *Swan Lake*; she is just as good in modern ballets; she knows how to act; she has a perfect dancer's body (with a lovely long neck); her technique is so strong that she can do anything a choreographer asks her to do; and she *looks* like a ballerina. Cynthia will very likely turn into a *prima ballerina*. The old-time ballerinas, the ballerina stars of today, and the brand-new ballerinas are very, very important to ballet. They not only make ballet beautiful and exciting, but they make, as we have seen, ballet history.

Above, Lawrence Rhodes and Lone Isaksen in a very modern ballet, *After Eden*, a fantasy about Adam and Eve after they were expelled from the Garden. *Facing page*, Cynthia Gregory and Ivan Nagy dance *The Eternal Idol*, a ballet suggested by the sculptures of Rodin. This photograph was made in a ballet studio while the ballet was being choreographed by Michael Smuin, so it is really a picture of ballet in the making.

Index

Note: italicized page numbers indicate illustrations.